150 Best Apartment Ideas

150 Best Apartment Ideas

COLLINS DESIGN

An Imprint of HarperCollins Publishers

150 BEST APARTMENT IDEAS
Copyright © 2006 by COLLINS DESIGN and LOFT Publications

HarperCollins books may be purchased for educational, business, or sales promotional use.
For information, please write: Special Markets Department, HarperCollins*Publishers*,
10 East 53rd Street, New York, NY 10022.

First published in 2007 by:
Collins Design,
An Imprint of HarperCollins*Publishers*
10 East 53rd Street
New York, NY 10022
Tel.: (212) 207-7000
Fax: (212) 207-7654
collinsdesign@harpercollins.com
www.harpercollins.com

Distributed throughout the world by:
HarperCollins*Publishers*
10 East 53rd Street
New York, NY 10022
Fax: (212) 207-7654

Executive editor:
Paco Asensio

Editorial coordination:
Ana Cañizares

Art director:
Mireia Casanovas Soley

Graphic design and layout:
Emma Termes

Library of Congress Control Number:

150 Best Apartment Ideas / [editorial coordination, Ana Cañizares]. — 1st ed.
p. cm.

ISBN-13: 978-0-06-113973-4
1. Apartments. 2. Interior architecture. 3. Interior decoration. I.
Cañizares, Ana Cristina G. II. Title: One hundred fifty best apartment ideas.

NA7860.A15 2006
728'.314--dc22

2006024121

Printed in China

Fourth Printing, 2009

Contents

Introduction

The existence of the apartment is inextricably tied to the history of urban settlements and their persistent growth since the onset of industrialization. As a type of residence, the apartment offers a practical and comfortable refuge in the city. The urban lifestyle can be as stimulating as it can be stressful, and it can take a toll on both body and mind. For this reason, making a haven out of home is perhaps the most effective antidote for the potential downfalls of a cosmopolitan lifestyle. The object is to create a genuine retreat in which to fully disconnect and relax. An apartment, no matter how small it is or where it is located, can be configured to make the most of its possibilities in relation to light, space and views, and if properly conceived, it can result in a dwelling that serves not only as a physical shelter but also as a welcoming space that invites repose. A myriad of techniques are available today to make the most of often limited apartment space, including the manipulation of light, surface area, ceiling height and floor levels, and the choice of materials, colors and textures. By introducing multifunctional furnishings and layouts, an apartment can also easily incorporate a home office or studio. In this book, we offer hundreds of fresh ideas drawn from a truly impressive selection of apartment spaces around the world designed by local and international architects and designers who, in each case, have managed to consolidate the needs of their clients with innovative strategies and solutions for contemporary living. With an array of apartment grouped according to type, *150 Best Apartment Ideas* serves as a concise and useful to both homeowners and designers in search of the perfect sanctuary within the city.

Single-Story

Ritz Mansions Apartment

Architect: Fiona Winzar
Architects
Location: Melbourne, Australia
Date of construction: 2005
Photography: Shania Shegedyn

Used for 15 years as an independent radio station, this space was refurbished by the new owners to return it to its original use as a residential apartment. In response to the long and irregular space, the designers created an open layout to maximize light and views, with the communal areas closest to the apartment's main source of daylight.

The masculine qualities of the construction are balanced by feminine elements, such as the delicate latticed screens and the curving patterns that decorate the space.

Plan

Fasan Residence

This 5,900-square-foot apartment is characterized by an uncluttered and fluid space generated by the elimination of excess walls and partitions. A sculptural and angled opening in the main wall connects the living area with the bathroom and kitchen, giving the apartment a unique, robust character.

Architect: Johannes Will/Willl
Manufaktur Architektur
Moebelkultur
Location: Vienna, Austria
Date of construction: 2004
Photography: Paul Ott

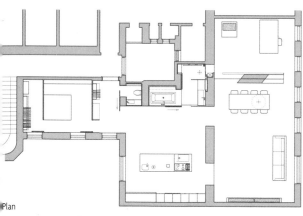

Plan

Using glass to separate
functional areas can add
depth to the space. Here, it
also defies the conventional
notions of privacy in the
bathroom.

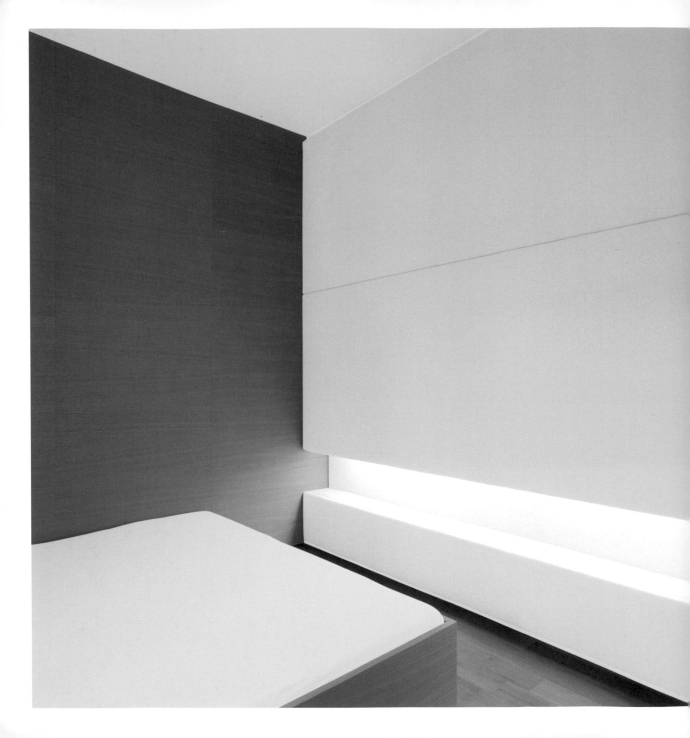

Pure lines, neutral colors and
smooth textures produce
an austere and elegant
atmosphere in this bathroom.

This building had been a hotel and, more recently, a photographic studio, before being acquired by the current owners. The main goal was to let in as much light as possible, improve air circulation, and take full advantage of the high ceilings. Translucent sliding panels, clerestory windows and an open layout produce a refreshing and inviting atmosphere.

Architect: Alden Maddry
Location: New York, NY, USA
Date of construction: 2005
Photography: Seong Kwon

The kitchen countertop doubles as a breakfast bar. The addition of comfortable barstools, produces an informal dining area.

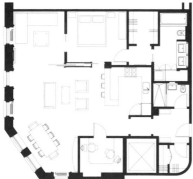

Plan

An extension of the living room, separated from the main space by resin panels, can be transformed into a guest bedroom that enjoys complete privacy.

Flatiron Apartment

Created for a fashion designer with a keen interest in the history of industrial design, this apartment was conceived as an open-plan and light-filled interior. The architect introduced translucent screens, mobile furnishings and neutral colors to achieve this. Materials such as wood, acrylic and recycled paper have produced a simple yet elegant space.

Architect: James Slade/Slade Architecture
Location: New York, NY, USA
Date of construction: 2003
Photography: Jordi Miralles

The acrylic-and-wood panels are similar to the Shoji screen used in Japanese dwellings, creating a fusion between Eastern and Western design.

Plan

A mobile storage unit set on wheels makes for a flexible kitchen layout and adds another countertop.

The selection of an unusual
material can result in a
striking design. This onyx sink
is lit from within to produce
an attractive visual effect.

New York Apartment

This residence was designed to accentuate available light and open space, using glass doors and partitions to separate the living areas from the bedrooms. Custom-made walnut furnishings contrast with stainless steel elements and warm fabrics. The kitchen opens onto the living area to create an integrated place for informal gatherings.

Architect: Stefania
Rinaldi/Studio Rinaldi
Location: New York, NY, USA
Date of construction: 2004
Photography: Wade Zimmerman

Large decorative pieces can make a strong visual statement. The pottery, left, and the painting and chandelier, right, add jolts of color.

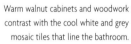

Warm walnut cabinets and woodwork
contrast with the cool white and grey
mosaic tiles that line the bathroom.

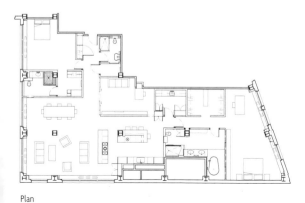

Plan

A small niche can be fitted out as an intimate dressing table or as a place to display decorative objects.

Unit P-18A

Located in an old building that formerly housed a department store, this apartment was endowed with especially high ceilings yet was limited by a fragmented layout. In addition to eliminating walls from the floor plan, the architects focused on scale, light and movement that would allow colors and materials to bring a new sense of richness and texture to the interior.

Architect: John Friedman Alice
Kimm Architects
Location: New York, NY, USA
Date of construction: 2002
Photography: Michael Moran

Simple furnishings and bare
walls can enhance the sense
of spaciousness and light.

Barcelona Apartment

This apartment in Barcelona takes advantage of its elongated floor plan to create a series of successive functional areas inundated by natural light. Furnishings and plants are incorporated into the design to differentiate the living spaces. They also alter the ambience, creating a tropical atmosphere within an urban apartment located on the top floor of a residential building in the heart of the city.

Architect: Helena Stanic
Location: Barcelona, Spain
Date of construction: 2004
Photography: Gogortza/Llorella

Japanese-style tatami bed can be raised from the floor by putting it on a wooden platform that also functions as a bedside table.

Plain sliding doors can be used to reveal or conceal an in-suite bathroom right next to the bed.

Los Angeles Apartment

This apartment is situated in one of L.A.'s historic Gas Company buildings constructed in 1924. These were later renovated as modern apartments. Polished concrete, bleached wood and an open-plan layout emphasize the clarity of the new interiors. Tall windows and light materials add a sense of luminosity.

Architect: Kerry Joyce
Associates
Location: Los Angeles, CA, USA
Date of construction: 2004
Photography: Dominique
Vorillon

The use of white throughout an entire space can produce an attractive and striking visual effect, if carefully maintained.

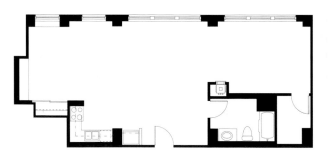

Plan

For a more subtle effect, light wood and neutral tones can be combined to create a soothing atmosphere.

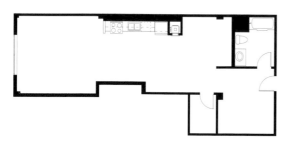

Plan

Mirrors can function as
decorative elements that
reflect the surrounding colors
and create a sense of depth.

Apartment in Berlin

Situated inside a new apartment building in the historic center of Berlin, this apartment explores new ways of integrating the conventional functions of a traditional household. Composed of various parallel volumes that channel light into the interior, the apartment incorporates mobile panels that allow the space to be configured in different ways.

Architect: Abcarius & Burns
Architecture Design
Location: Berlin, Germany
Date of construction: 2004
Photography: Ludger Paffrath

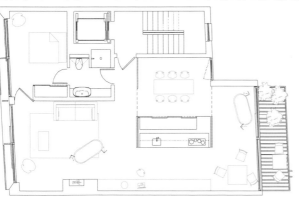

Plan

Full-height sliding glass doors join the living area with the terrace, allowing the dining table to be easily moved outside for alfresco meals and gatherings.

Residence in Bogotá

Architect: Guillermo Arias
& Luis Cuartas
Location: Bogotá, Colombia
Date of construction: 2001
Photography: Eduardo
Consuegra & Pablo Rojas

This residence occupies a large part of what was once a traditional, multiroom apartment were in a building dating back to the 1930s. Located on the top floor, the rooms were redesigned and modified in various ways in order to enrich the space. By making use of various lines of sight and letting in as much natural light as possible, the architects achieved a more fluid and practical scheme.

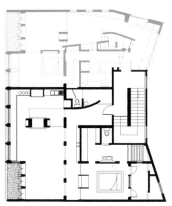

Plans

A partition wall in the kitchen area serves multiple purposes. A spce divider, it also holds a fireplace and storage for dry goods and utensils.

Two sinks in different shapes add a custom touch to this antique-inspired contemporary bathroom.

N House

This elegant two-bedroom apartment is divided into distinct areas by means of panels and partitions that create unusual and versatile spaces. A glass wall framed by a white boxlike structure visually links the dining area and living room, while a slatted wooden screen sets apart the entrance from the dining space. The predominant use of white underscores the open character of the floor plan.

Architect: Studio Damilano
Location: Cuneo, Italy
Date of construction: 2003
Photography: Michele de Vita

The partition, reminescent
of a picture frame, lends
a theatrical touch, as if
watching the space through
a television screen or as
part of a stage set.

An elevated platform
provides space for a sunken
bathtub and plenty of
surface area for toiletries
and decorative objects.

Originally a six-room apartment located in the center of Vienna, this residence was converted into an open-plan space for both living and working. Interior walls were demolished and the divisions between the bathroom, kitchen and bedroom were created along a single, red wall, integrating contemporary elements within the building's original footprint.

Architect: Lakonis Architekten
Location: Vienna, Austria
Date of construction: 2003
Photography: Margherita
Spiluttini

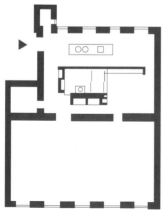

Plan

Niches within walls provide
tidy storage areas which are
used as shelves for books and
other objects.

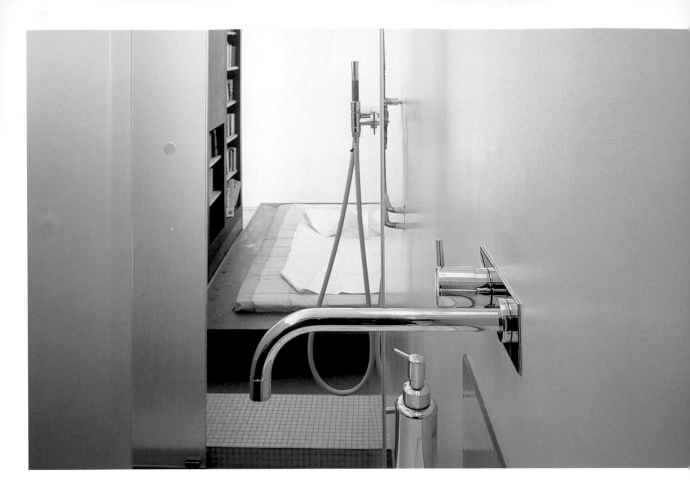

Translucent glass provides
privacy within the shower,
while allowing natural light to
filter through the space.

Located in the north of Italy, this residence was transformed from a typically segmented apartment into an open, fluid space. It is characterized by a mixture of styles expressed by the choice furnishings and decorative elements. The main feature is a sliding glass panel with plant motifs that divides the living area from the studio and creates a colorful focal point.

Architect: CLS Architects
Location: Bergamo, Italy
Date of construction: 2004
Photography: Andrea
Martiradonna

The bedrooms feature a more subdued palette and virtually no decoration to achieve a greater sense of tranquillity and repose.

Milan Apartment

This apartment is located in a 1950s building and enjoys 360-degree views of the city. Its renovation entailed a careful survey of the original structure in order to complement elements such as the wooden furnishings, the kitchen mosaic, the marble floors and the sash windows along the entire length of the apartment.

Architect: **Carolina Nisivoccia**
Location: **Milan, Italy**
Date of construction: **2005**
Photography: **Paolo Riolzi**

An entire wall can be
designated as shelves for
storing books and magazines,
adopting different shapes to
create a more dynamic and
useful composition.

Another library opens up to reveal a guest bedroom, which becomes part of the living area when the doors remain open.

Select designer furnishings and vintage pieces from the fifties and sixties imbue this space with a sense of elegant design. The retro look is complemented by contemporary accessories and materials, such as stainless steel, Corian and resin floors—all of which enhance the glossy, glamorous atmosphere of this apartment in Milan.

Architect: Carlo Donati
Location: Milan, Italy
Date of construction: 2005
Photography: Paolo Riolzi

Linear elements contrast
with the curved forms of
some furnishings, lamps and
patterns featured on the
rugs and other decorative
objects.

The kitchen conceals most
of its storage space within
the freestanding module,
enabling the walls to
remain devoid of clutter.

The retro theme is present through the entire apartment, featuring chairs, telephones and radios original to this period. Such pieces give the space character.

Busto Arsizio Apartment

Designed for a young couple with a daughter, this contemporary apartment carefully uses light as a decorative element in addition to the materials and structures that comprise the project. The combination of rough materials, like unpolished concrete, and refined ones, like walnut, create a pleasing contrast that lends a feeling of originality to the space.

Architect: Daniele Geltrudi
Location: Milan, Italy
Date of construction: 2004
Photography: Andrea Martiradonna

Small square windows can be
found at different points
throughout the entire space,
serving as a source of light
and a strong visual element.

Plan

The decorative objects are few but significant. Unique pieces and clearly defined shapes provide a balanced composition of forms.

The architect created the
black stucco walls inside the
bathroom by applying several
layers of stucco using crossed
spatula strokes.

Via Pisani Apartment

Situated on the twenty-third floor of the only residential skyscraper in the city, this 3,750-square-foot apartment enjoys 180-degree views of the urban landscape. The interior was conceived as a box within a box, utilizing glass partitions that enclose the daytime areas in the heart of the floor plan.

Architect: Fabio Azzolina
Location: Milan, Italy
Date of construction: 2005
Photography: Andrea Martiradonna

Tinted glass can create a
highly sophisticated look and
add a new dimension to any
interior space.

Plan

A simple design achieves an elegant atmosphere through the combination of antique pieces and contemporary elements. The open and continuous layout is adorned with original lamp fixtures that define the different areas of the apartment— organized so that the daytime areas receive the most amount of daylight.

Architect: Luca Rolla
Location: Milan, Italy
Date of construction: 2004
Photography: Andrea
Martiradonna

Opting for a round window in place of a more conventional one contributes an unusual feature to this kitchen.

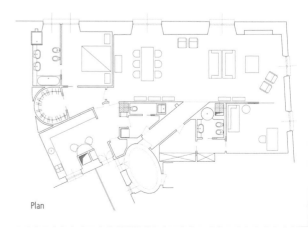

Plan

Bonanova Residence

Previously carved into two garages, this 1,500-square-foot space was transformed into one residential apartment in Barcelona. A double-glazed façade eliminates exterior noise while allowing for abundant daylight and views of the city. The layout is centered on a cube that contains the bedrooms. Around these are the living, kitchen and dining areas.

Architect: Francesc Rifé
Location: Barcelona, Spain
Date of construction: 2005
Photography: Eugeni Pons

Plan

By situating the private areas in the center of the layout, the daytime areas can receive the maximum available natural light.

Two bathrooms are located at the rear of the apartment, one of which is part of the master bedroom suite and is connected to a courtyard.

This small apartment required a gut renovation on a tight budget to accommodate a young couple. In response to the limited space available, the design aims to optimize surface area while enhancing the perception of spaciousness. An efficient layout and a new full-height opening leading to the sleeping area allow the occupants to see the viewsthrough the windows from both the living area and the bedroom.

Architect: Roy Leone
Design Studio
Location: New York, NY, USA
Date of construction: 2005
Photography: Mikiko Kikuyama

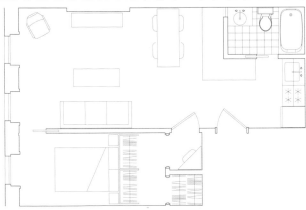

Plan

Right: A tall, narrow
sandblasted-glass window
brings light into the
bathroom.

Pink House

Situated inside a mansion dating to 1950, this apartment was renovated based on its original structure, which housed an irregular geometric plan. Simple design solutions were integrated, using varying ceiling heights and transparent materials, and the distribution of furnishings and color to differentiate the spaces and highlight the original floor plan.

Architect: Filippo Bombace
Location: Rome, Italy
Date of construction: 2004
Photography: Luigi Filetici

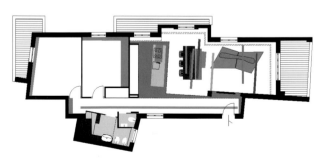

Plan

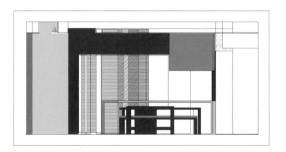

Section

Strips of light are integrated into this tabletop, creating a dynamic interplay of color and geometric forms with surrounding elements of similar shaped color.

This seaside apartment displays an urban-chic style within a relatively small space. Lighting and storage techniques that maintain an uncluttered atmosphere achieve this effect. From the entrance, a corridor leads to a small room in which large closets are concealed behind wooden panels. The seemingly spacious living room shares space with the kitchen and the dining area.

Architect: UdA
Location: Nice, France
Date of construction: 2001
Photography: Heiko Semeyer

Full-height screens diffuse
intense sunlight and provide
adequate privacy with a
minimal and elegant gesture.

Plan

Placing this bed lengthwise allowed the addition of large window. A shelf underneath the window doubles as a bedside table.

Apartment Veen

A classic apartment from the 1930s was turned into a contemporary living space with dynamic spatial relationships. The central entrance hall—the most important feature of the original apartment—was the key ingredient of the design. Through its transformation into a more abstract space, the architects achieved a completely renewed interior.

Architect: **Moriko Kira**
Location: **Amsterdam, Netherlands**
Date of construction: **2004**
Photography: **Christian Richters**

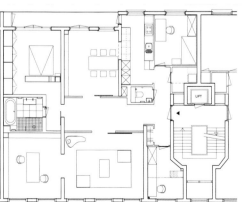

Plan

Traditional doors were replaced with large openings fitted with sliding doors in different color combinations to create a dramatic effect.

New openings were created
in order to establish a visual
connection and a more
abstract relationship between
the different areas.

Residence in São Paulo

This Brazilian residence was previously a conventional apartment with four distinctly divided bedrooms. The new scheme comprises two large bedrooms and an integrated living area. Large pivoting doors serve as dividing panels that link or separate the private and public areas. The living area is defined by a dark-wood bookcase that wraps around and envelops the perimeter of the space.

Architect: Arthur Casas
Location: São Paulo, Brazil
Date of construction: 2003
Photography: Tuca Reines

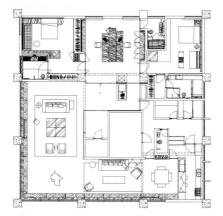

Plan

When open, the pivoting
doors appear to be panels,
creating the sensation of a
more open and fluid space.

La Magdalena Apartment

The plan for this project called for a fully integrated space, with the living area and bedroom located in what was originally the main living room space. A white wooden structure unobtrusively divides these two areas and doubles as a bookcase, television cabinet and music center. Simple white walls contrast with a vividly colored kitchen with open storage and a decidedly rustic touch.

Architect: Guillermo Arias
Location: Bogotá, Colombia
Date of construction: 2002
Photography: Pablo Rojas
& Álvaro Gutiérrez

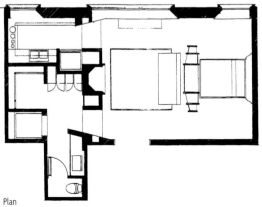

Plan

Although separate from the living area, the kitchen's open character allows interaction between cooks and guests.

Antique-style taps are combined with custom-designed lamp fixtures to preserve the original character of the apartment.

Designed by the owner, this apartment makes use of subtle contrasts to create a relaxed and sophisticated interior. Light colors chosen for the walls and most of the furnishings contrast with the dark oak floors, while a mixture of styles creates a cosmopolitan atmosphere. The simple floor plan allows for a spacious living area, kitchen, bedroom and bathroom with an office niche.

Architect: Benn Haitsma
Location: London, UK
Date of construction: 2005
Photography: Carlos Domínguez

46

The architect took advantage
of a niche in the bedroom to
create a small working area,
adapting the table and shelves
to fit the curved wall.

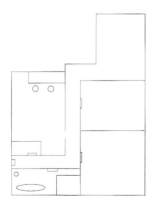

Plan

The use of mirrors creates
the illusion of space to make
small areas like bathrooms
seem larger.

McGrath Apartment

This apartment in Chelsea was transformed into an elegant and practical living space. The elongated floor plan was modified by eliminating walls in order to achieve a more flexible and fluid space. Sliding doors emphasize the linear qualities and vertical nature of the design, while a monochromatic palette emphasizes the continuity between the different functional areas.

Architect: Anima
Location: New York, NY, USA
Date of construction: 2003
Photography: Paul Rivera/Archphoto

Integrated taps and shelves
save space and maintain a
tidy kitchen. The use of
stainless steel throughout the
kitchen complements the
apartment's minimalist design.

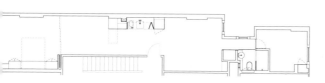

an

Xiangshan Apartment

This apartment stands out for its elegant and timeless Asian-style interior, characterized by a variety of textures, materials and dark tones. Raw gray granite, sheets of stainless steel and rusted metals define the general look of the home and the overall design imbue with a sleek, contemporary edge.

Architect: Hank M. Chao/Mohen Design
Location: Shanghai, China
Date of construction: 2005
Photography: Moder Chou

Plan

A raw-metal wall at the entrance leads to the living spaces, which are separated by a large interior bamboo garden.

50

The intense contrast between light and dark in this apartment lends a dramatic and seductive look.

A pivoting door opens to reveal a path that leads to the private areas of the apartment.

A curved partition changes this small space into a comfortable residence. The most remarkable feature is the ceiling, which partially exposes the original structure of the building through an oval-shaped composition of foam panels. It also integrates an indirect lighting system that produces an abstract, futuristic effect.

Architect: Morris Sato Studio
Location: New York, NY, USA
Date of construction: 2005
Photography: Michael Moran

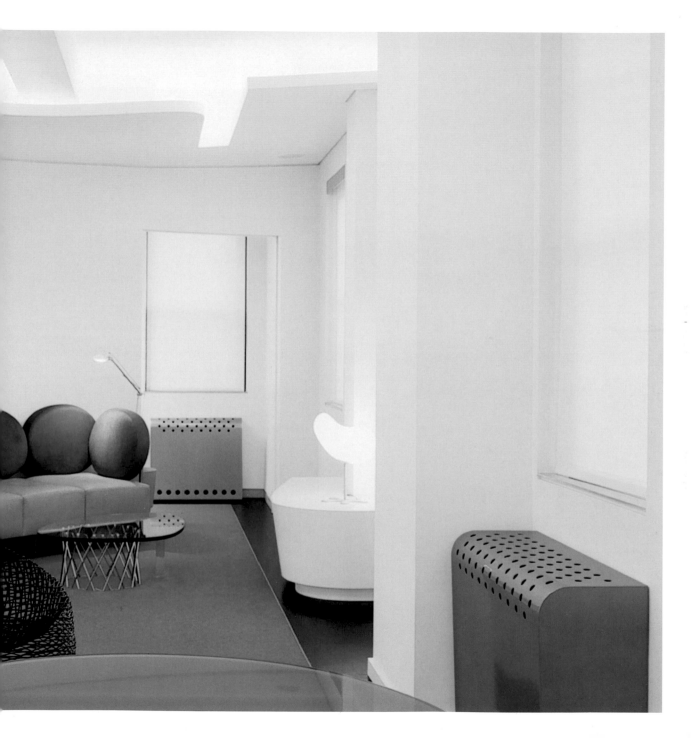

Straight lines and curved edges make up this abstract composition of foam panels that decorate the ceiling.

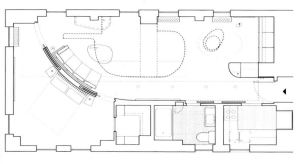

Plan

The colorful palette combines
crisp blue and green
throughout the apartment,
imparting a cool and
minimalist aesthetic.

Situated within a residential building designed by the renowned architect Renzo Piano, this apartment is characterized by spacious living areas and privileged views of Sydney's bay. A large living, kitchen and dining area are followed by a series of bedrooms situated along a corridor. Glasspanes in the immense window wall open and close to provide natural ventilation.

Architect: Tobias Partners
Location: Sydney, Australia
Date of construction: 2006
Photography: Murray Fredericks

The glass façade is designed
with an integrated louver
system that opens and closes
panes to allow cool breezes in.

A small room within the main living space was designated as an office and library where the occupants can work.

Brondesbury Villas

Measuring only 700 square feet, this apartment was converted chiefly by relocating the bathroom and kitchen to provide a better view of the back garden upon entering the space. The living room wall was opened to create continuity with the bedroom, which connects to a bathroom fitted with a full-length mirror on one side to visually enlarge the small space.

Architect: Esther Hagenlocher,
Sabine Storp, Patrick Weber
Location: **London, UK**
Date of construction: **2006**
Photography: **Nina Siber**

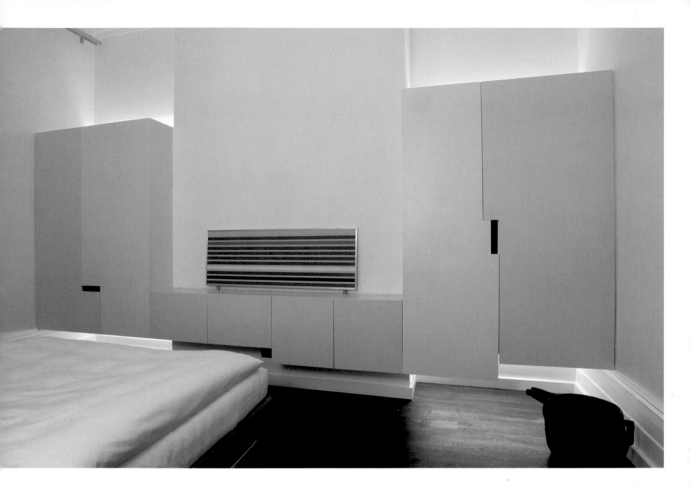

The closets in the bedroom
stop well short of the floor to
keep the space clear for an
uncluttered effect.

Architect Brunete Fraccaroli was commissioned to design this 5,900-square-foot apartment to suit the modern and dynamic lifestyle as a top executive. A combination of materials, such as glass, steel and wood are complemented by high-tech features like automatic sliding doors. A central panel divides the bedroom from the living area and integrates a pivoting plasma TV.

Architect: **Brunete Fraccaroli**
Location: **São Paulo, Brazil**
Date of construction: **2002**
Photography: **Tuca Reinés**

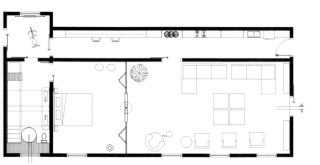

Plan

Colored lights can add a
dramatic touch to any kitchen
when combined with the right
materials and finishes.

This bathroom was conceived as a shrine
to personal pampering and also
incorporates a small gym.

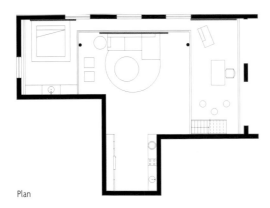

Plan

Sempacher Apartments

This residential building located in Zurich is an example of modern and sustainable urban renovation. The innovative project incorporates a flexible structure that allows future generations to modify the interior spaces while maintaining a harmonious dialogue with the exterior. The apartments are characterized by open areas and the generous use of glass.

Architect: Camenzind Evolution
Location: Zurich, Switzerland
Date of construction: 2004
Photography: Camenzind
Evolution

57

The front incorporates a
shading system with vertical
screens that cover the
balconies.

Stainless steel balconies create a
pleasing contrast to the natural wood
floors and ceilings.

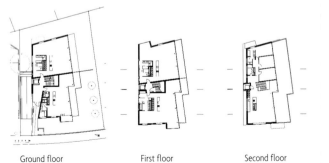

Ground floor   First floor   Second floor

A utility core contains the
kitchen and bathroom,
allowing the living areas to
enjoy more space and light.

Duplex

Mp3 Residence

Designed for a young actor in search of a dynamic and sensual residence, this previously cluttered residence was opened up and space redistributed, resulting 1in an open and luminous apartment. Throughout the two-and-a-half-story volume, frosted glass panels were introduced to separate the different environments.

Architect: Michel Rojkind
& Simon Hamui
Location: Mexico DF, Mexico
Date of construction: 2005
Photography: Jaime Navarro

The distribution of functional areas over open levels increases the sensation of space, visually links the areas and creates a dynamic relationship between the dwelling and its occupant.

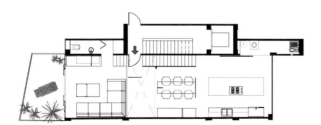
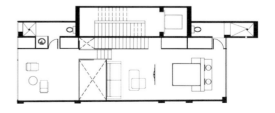

Plans

This elegant and modern one-bedroom duplex is located in the Born quarter of Barcelona. The layout distributes the hall, kitchen, living room and dining area on the lower level, and it places the master bedroom and bathroom upstairs. Shades of white contrasted with glossy and matte black elements to create a striking, sophisticated ambience.

Architect: Joan Pons Forment
Location: Barcelona, Spain
Date of construction: 2005
Photography: Jordi Miralles

A sculptural kitchen conceals all utensils and food, and it becomes a decorative element in doing so.

The upper level of the duplex
wraps around the central void
to accommodate the bed on
one side and a comfortable
working area on the other.

Apartment in Mexico

This apartment is one of the six contained within a residential building, which also houses a contemporary art gallery. Each apartment occupies an entire floor and is the beneficiary of an open plan space in which the tenants can organize the living areas according to their specific needs and desires.

Architect: Ten Arquitectos
Location: Mexico DF, Mexico
Date of construction: 2005
Photography: Jaime Navarro

62

Double-height spaces, sliding
doors and full-length windows
maximize the daylight and
views on the interior of
the dwelling.

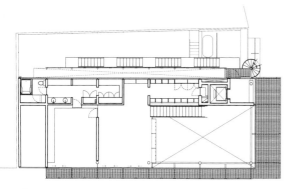

Plan

Fraternitat Duplex

Simplicity and color are the characteristic features of this duplex apartment, which integrates a mezzanine level to accommodate the living room. Red, white and black give the furnishings and structural elements a bold appearance, and skylights on the top level wash the lounge area with plenty of daylight.

Architect: Joan Bach
Location: Barcelona, Spain
Date of construction: 2003
Photography: Jordi Miralles

Two stools pulled up to the
L-shaped kitchen counter
create an informal dining area
for breakfast.

The tiles chosen for the bathroom match the color used for the bedroom walls, creating continuity between these adjacent areas.

Apartment in São Paulo

In refurbishing this apartment, the architect preserved the original iron beam structure and worked in a mezzanine, which houses the owner's office and master bedroom. The lower floor comprises the living room, kitchen and a small media room for listening to music and watching films.

Architect: Brunete Fraccaroli
Location: São Paulo, Brazil
Date of construction: 2003
Photography: João Ribeiro

The original brick walls create
a warm contrast to the
tempered-glass panels, which
are used for the mezzanine
structure, allowing continuity
and transparency between
both levels.

Private Apartment

Architect: Paskin Kyriakides
Sands Architects
Location: London, UK
Date of construction: 2004
Photography: Paskin Kyriakides
Sands Architects

The original layout of this building was ideal for creating urban living spaces on multiple levels, resulting in unique, modern apartments with fine details and finishes. The layout of the interior spaces make the most of both the structural and lighting conditions that already existed before the renovation.

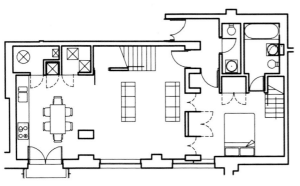

Plan

Lightweight staircases flanked by glass railings create a subtl differentiation between the tw levels. White walls contrast with abundant wood and stainless steel surfaces.

67

The bathrooms each possess a unique character due to the materials used and the contemporary fittings.

Duplex Kang

This project consists of a duplex renovation located on a busy street in Taipei. The elongated and narrow surface area of the space was revamped by introducing a frosted-glass panel on the rear wall and painting the walls, floors and ceiling in white to generate continuity, structure and luminosity.

Architect: Shi-Chieh
Lu/CJ Studio
Location: Taipei, Taiwan
Date of construction: 2004
Photography: Kuomin Lee

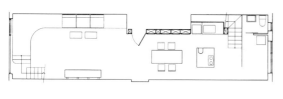

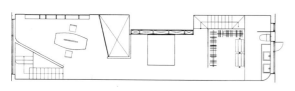

Plans

68

A shelf along the floor rises off the ground becoming the staircase that leads to the mezzanine level.

The transparent staircase
filters light throughout the
space, while the extensive use
of white further emphasizes
the calm, airy feeling.

Velluto Apartment

A central courtyard is at the core of this duplex in Milan. Living spaces and bedrooms revolve around this central source of daylight, benefiting from the peace and tranquillity generated by this layout. The living area, further enhanced by a double-height void above it, looks onto the upper levels of the apartment.

Architect: Ferruccio Laviani
Location: Milan, Italy
Date of construction: 2004
Photography: Paolo Riolzi

70

By creating a central
courtyard, an apartment can
obtain natural daylight
without having to face the
main street.

Circulation areas are used as
exhibition walls to display
large paintings and other
favorite works of art.

Architect: Luca Rolla
Location: Milan, Italy
Date of construction: 2005
Photography: Andrea
Martiradonna

This apartment was designed as a live-in studio for a working woman who wanted a comfortable living space where she could work and receive friends when visiting Milan. A single open space divided by partitions, which feature cutouts that visually link the areas behind them. A metal staircase leads to an upper level that has as a guest room and walk-in closet.

Plan

Partitions that stop short of
the ceiling create a more fluid
perception of space and allow
light to pass through the
different areas.

The studio is behind one of the partitions and provides a quiet, spacious working area.

Rote Wand Apartment

Located in a small city in Austria, this apartment occupies a building that used to house a hotel. Built in the traditional local style, the building enjoys spectacular views of nearby mountains and a lush green landscape. The interior of the new living space preserves characteristic elements of the original structure, which serve as a conterpoint to a striking minimalist design.

Architect: Holz Box Tirol
Location: Zug, Lech am Arlberg, Austria
Date of construction: 2003
Photography: Bruno Klomfar

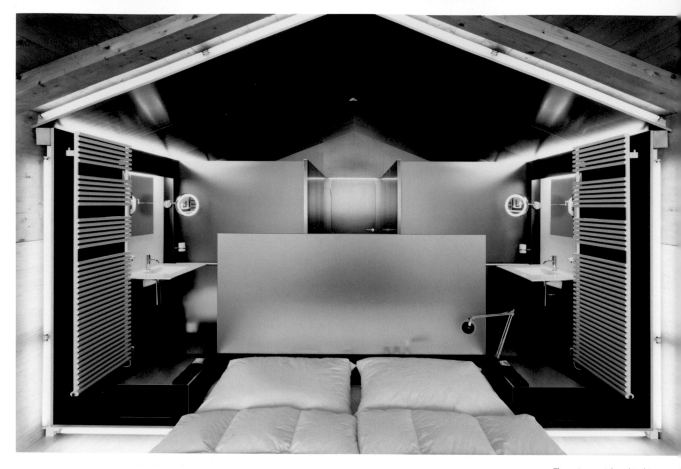

The main material used in this apartm
conversion was Finnish plywood
economic and versatile resou

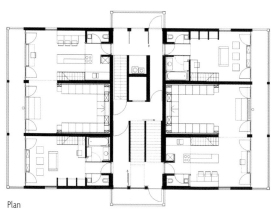

Plan

74

The rustic effect of the plywood is offset by the polished black surfaces that add a modern edge.

Section

In line with the modifications of the 1896 apartment building in the center of Munich, this residence was rebuilt and expanded for its current owner. By merging a basement and a first-floor apartment, a duplex was created that divides the living area from the sleeping area. The living area features an open-plan kitchen punctuated by a central fireplace.

Architect: Hofman
Dujardin Architecten
Location: Munich, Germany
Date of construction: 2005
Photography: Uli Gohs

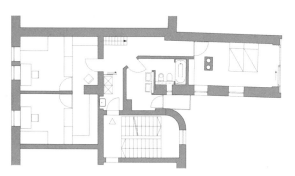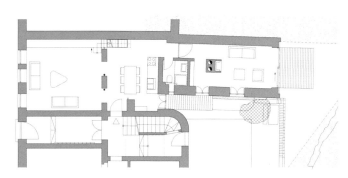

Plans

75

The staircase leading to the
sleeping level integrates a
seamless arrangement of
closets to provide extra
storage space.

The challenge of this apartment renovation lay in endowing this previously dark and poorly lit space with abundant light. The architects took advantage of the existing skylights and windows and created a sculptural, glacierlike structure that absorbs light into the living spaces. Seamless finishes make for uncluttered spaces, while gaps filled with artificial light illuminate the "glacier" at night.

Architect: Gus Wüstemann
Location: Lucerne, Switzerland
Date of construction: 2005
Photography: Bruno Helbling

The straight edges of the
architecture are softened by
the curved forms of the
furnishings and lamps.

Plan

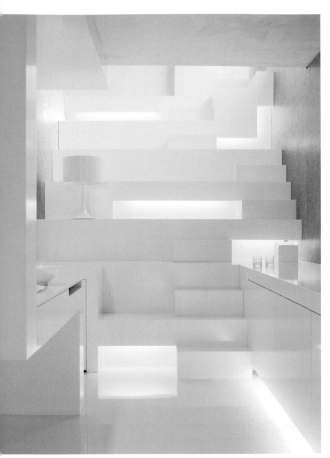

Open-steps leading to the rooftop terrace are on one side of wide risers. Sculptural openings channel daylight into the living space.

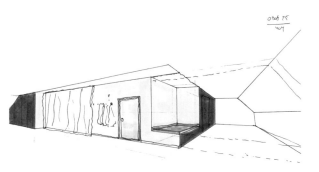

Sketch

The glossy resin floors recall a frozen
lake, bouncing off both natural and
artificial light in all directions.

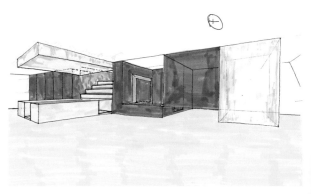

Sketch

A3-3 Apartment

Esconsed in what was previously a school that dates to 1932, this residence is one of three new apartments created within the existing space. The architects explored the possibilities of tearing down the old walls and inserting open spaces to generate dynamic spatial relationships between the various levels that in the apartment.

Architect: NAT Architecten
Location: Eindhoven,
Netherlands
Date of construction: 2005
Photography: Peter Cuypers

78

A central, double-height
volume contains the living
areas, which are infused with
an airy, well-lit atmosphere.

Plans

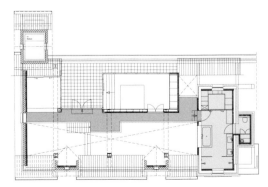

The living room and kitchen are visually linked by a spectacular aquarium in the wall that acts as a window to both sides.

The aquarium also extends into the
bathroom for an unexpected and serene
viewing experience.

Great Portland Street Apartment

This apartment is a former assembly hall situated within a 1920s building in central London. The existing 18-foot-high space now contains the living area, kitchen, bar and private film-screening room beyond. From here, a series of glass-fronted elements that project out from the upper level provide interior views of the bedroom that lies behind.

Architect: **Eldridge Smerin**
Location: **London, UK**
Date of construction: **2004**
Photography: **Lyndon Douglas**

80

To avoid introducing any load borne by the lower level, each projecting element consists of a separate structure hung from a steel beam concealed above the ceiling.

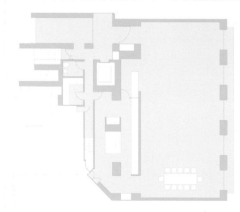

Plan

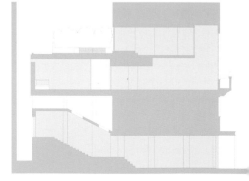

Section

Apartment in Chicago

This impressive Chicago residence is located on the fifty-eighth and fifty-ninth floors of a Michigan Avenue high-rise dominated by views of the John Hancock Tower. The duplex, once a single space, was divided into recreational and functional areas defined by the use of specific materials. Metal was chosen for the lower level, and wood for the upper level.

Architect: Valerio Dewalt
Train Associates
Location: Chicago, IL, USA
Date of construction: 2001
Photography: Barbara Karant

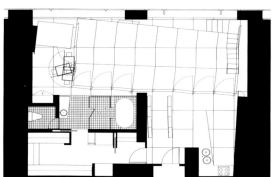

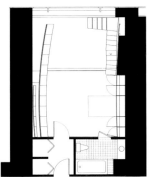

Plans

81

A pivoting wall allows the
bathroom to remain open to
the bedroom or be enclosed
for greater privacy.

Loft Apartments

Loft One

Architect: Leonardo
Annecca/L-A-Design
Location: New York, NY, USA
Date of construction: 2005
Photography: Miaz Brothers,
Michael Greag

This live-work apartment in Manhattan was conceived as a loft with a compact floor plan. It was implemented on a tight budget and with low-tech features that contrast with a high-density city such as New York. The design maximizes space by integrating all the basic living functions in a discreet, chic and unpretentious environment where artists and designers can both live and showcase their work.

82

The elongated space was transformed into a succession of continuous spaces divided into a work-exhibition area and a living-sleeping area.

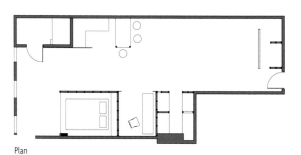

Plan

83

Translucent fabrics are a
simple and attractive solution
for delineating distinct areas
within a single space.

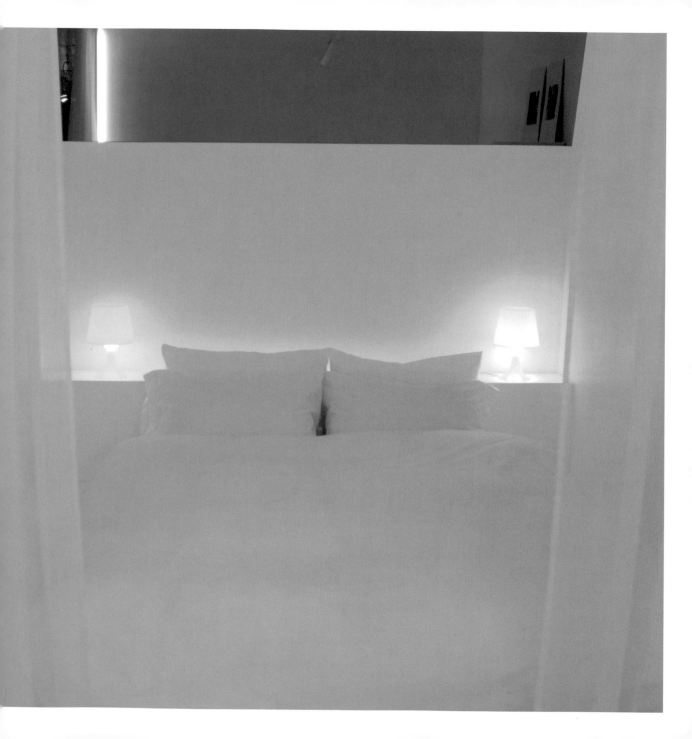

McCollum Loft

Architect: Roy Leone
Design Studio
Location: New York, NY, USA
Date of construction: 2003
Photography: Eduard
Hueber/Archphoto

Located in Manhattan's SoHo district inside a typical nineteenth century building, this apartment features characteristic period details like steel columns which have been painted white to soften their industrial feel. The sleeping area, integrated into the single space, is fitted with a ceiling rail onto which a curtain can be fixed in order to isolate the bed from the remaining space.

Plan

84

The presence of the steel columns was used to distinguish the kitchen from the dining area.

85

The bathroom is the only area that can be closed off by a full length door, fabricated from translucent glass to keep a sense of visual continuity.

Frankie Loft

This loft-style apartment is a perfect example of how to distribute space effectively with beautiful results. High ceilings leave room for an elevated bed structure in order to provide a spacious living area underneath and a small working area. Simple furnishings in vivid colors highlight the different areas, while the large windows filter abundant light into the space.

Architect: Joan Bach
Location: Barcelona, Spain
Date of construction: 2004
Photography: Jordi Miralles

86

The bathroom is next to the kitchen, the result of grouping the services areas together for efficiency.

Flinders Lane Apartment

Located within an old office building, this space was converted into a residential apartment for a young bachelor. The space is primarily defined by a multifunctional, free-standing wood-framed unit that encloses the sleeping area, provides storage space and serves as an additional dining area. The structure also incorporates bookshelves and comprises strong visual elements.

Architect: Staughton Architects
Location: Melbourne, Australia
Date of construction: 2001
Photography: Shannon McGrath

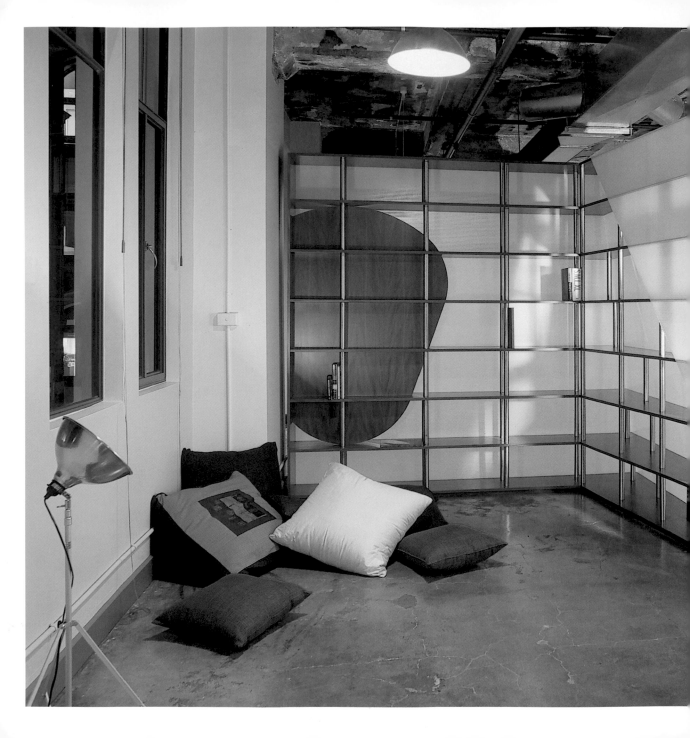

87

Black and white tiles offer
striking contrast and a sense
of depth in the discrete
bathroom space.

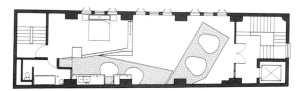

Plan

Architect: James Slade/Slade
Architecture
Location: New York, NY, USA
Date of construction: 2003
Photography: Jordi Miralles

Designed for a young photographer couple, this apartment had to accommodate a light table and a sizable filing cabinet among the essential elements of their living space. To maximize the daylight filtering into the living areas, the light table was placed farthest from the windows, alongside one of the lateral walls.

A dining table with spare benches instead of traditional chairs creates an uncluttered informal dining area within an open space.

The master suite boasts a bathroom partly enclosed by a frosted-glass panel that allows daylight to filter in.

Plan

Combining large tiles and
mosaic tiles can result in an
arresting composition when
it is done in neutral shades.

Egg Loft

Architect: Angelica Ruano, Pierre
Nicolas Ledoux/Plain Space
Location: New York, NY, USA
Date of construction: 2004
Photography: Paul
Rivera/Archphoto

A former office and commercial space, this apartment was divested of its segmented layout and low ceilings in favor of an open plan. At the core of the new layout is an oval, slotted-wood structure with a lounge area, which is a beacon of texture and colorin the subdued minimalist interior. Intense colored light bleeds through the slots to make a strong visual statement within the space.

Plan

The lighting inside the oval structure changes hue to create a dynamic and ongoing interplay of color and mood throughout the day.

The oval also marks the
curves of a hallway that leads
to a completely unadorned,
open-plan bathroom with an
elliptical bathtub form.

Womb

A multifunctional home and office space, Womb—an acronym for work, office, home and base—represents the recognition that a dwelling must fulfill a variety of needs. The modular space is designed to be four rooms in one, which can be altered to be as elemental or complex as necessary through a series of automated elements and pivoting furniture and cabinetry.

Architect: Johnson Chou
Location: Toronto, Canada
Date of construction: 2003
Photography: Volker Seding
Photography

92

The living area contains a bed that disappears into the floor when not in use, allowing a cantilevered couch to fold out from the wall.

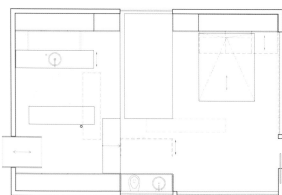

Plan

A U-shaped wall conceals the bathroom. When the room is not in use, the wall automatically closes against the fixtures to regain the space lost when unoccupied.

This enormous 14,500-square-foot apartment boasts the industrial qualities of a genuine loft space. Structural steel pillars were painted over in white, integrating them into an elegant and minimalist interior design characterized by designer furnishings in neutral shades. Red was used as an accent color, while narrow slots in the ceiling simulate skylights.

Architect: A-cero Arquitectos
Location: Madrid, Spain
Date of construction: 2005
Photography: Santiago Barro

93

The dining area is differentiated from the living area by a black rug that stands out against the white floor.

The austere black kitchen surfaces are interrupted by only a white counter, creating a dramatic effect.

Van Beestraat Residence

The building that houses this apartment was used in the past as a horsestable, the as a tram shed, and later as a college for midwives. During the transformation into a residence the designer tried to preserve old architectual elements into the new design, which has the qualities of a loft but adopts a spatial distribution that seeks to maintain a great deal of privacy in the bedrooms.

Architect: Marc Prosman
Architecten
Location: Amsterdam,
Netherlands
Date of construction: 2004
Photography: Christian Richters

94

A wooden panel, which incorporates a sliding door separates the kitchen from the study and also isolates the master bedroom.

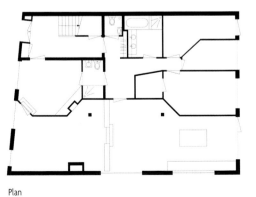

Plan

Apart from wood, glass is also used to
separate the different areas of the space.

Skylights are the main source
of light in the bathroom,
which is not located near any
of the main windows on the
outside wall.

Paris Apartment

Architect: Peter Tyberghien
Location: Paris, France
Date of construction: 2003
Photography: Alejandro
Bahamón

This compact and luxurious apartment was created for the purpose of receiving guests for short stays in Paris. A fully integrated layout combines living room, bedroom, kitchen and bath in one, making use of closets, levels, multifunctional elements and a glass panel that divides the bed from the large circular bath.

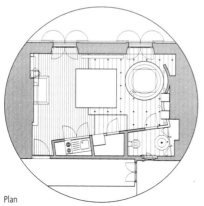

Plan

A series of folding doors
conceals a small kitchen,
closet and toilet. The latter
is the only enclosed space
within the apartment.

A liquid-crystal partition
becomes transparent or
translucent with the flip of a
switch, in order to provide
the free-standing bathtub with
greater privacy if needed.

Miami Beach Apartment

Conceived as a second residence for sporadic use, this apartment combines every household function into a single space. Polished-concrete floors and concrete pillars complement the Art Deco style of the building, and simple, contemporary furnishings make for a fresh, comfortable and attractive space.

Architect: Pablo Uribe
Location: Miami Beach, FL, USA
Date of construction: 2003
Photography: Claudia Uribe

Plan

The apartment is divided in two ha
The private areas, including the bedr
and bathroom, are one side, while
kitchen and living room are on the o

98

In warm climates, a partially enclosed shower can be the best solution for a unique bathing experience.

Ben Avigdor Apartment

Designed and built by Tel Aviv-based partnership U-I, (Avi Laiser and Amir Shwarz) this loft apartment was built in an old diamond-polishing factory that was vacant for more than a decade. The space is characterized by continuous polished-concrete floors, white walls and cabinets, and a colored wall, or box, that defines the different uses within the open space.

Architect: Avi Laiser
& Amir Shwarz
Location: Tel Aviv, Israel
Date of construction: 2005
Photography: Miri Davidovitch

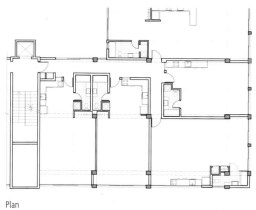

Plan

99

Few but distinctive pieces furnish the loft, allowing the industrial character of the space to show through.

Gershon Apartment

This inviting one-bedroom apartment emerged after a commercial space in New York's Flatiron District was remodeled. In joining the two extremities of the elongated plan, a central utility core was designed with wooden panels that conceal a storage area and an office. This wall acts as a link between living area and bedroom and also defines the kitchen.

Architect: Jeff Etelamaki
Design Studio
Location: New York, NY, USA
Date of construction: 2004
Photography: Steve Williams

Plan

100

Resembling Japanes shoji
screens, steel-framed
translucent panels reveal a
sleeping area that can be
integrated into the living area.

Architect: Manel
Torres/In Disseny
Location: Caldes de Montbui,
Spain
Date of construction: 2005
Photography: Stephan Zahring

Through the use of repeated color and furniture of a similare style, this apartment achieves a single, unified space with clearly differentiated areas. Red was chosen for certain walls to distinguish areas like the kitchen, dining room and bedroom. The living room is delineated by an open bookcase and can be separated from the bedroom by an elegant dark-wood sliding door.

The kitchen counter incorporates a slide-out element that serves as an auxiliary surface for placing drinks or preparing meals.

Loft in Vienna

Architect: Willl Manufaktur
Architektur Moebelkultur
Location: Vienna, Austria
Date of construction: 2003
Photography: Paul Ott

This 1,900-square-foot apartment is located in a nineteenth-century Viennese building. A subdued color palette and choice of high-quality materials reinforces the airy quality of the space, characterized by tall ceilings and bare white walls. The loftlike atmosphere also boasts an impressive kitchen bounded by glass walls and a spacious bedroom that lies behind a pivoting door.

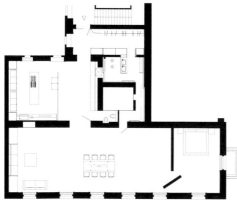

Plan

The elegance of a living space
is often determined by the
presence of a few high-quality
materials and fittings.

Escarmis Residence

Situated in the heart of the Barcelona's Gothic Quarter, this apartment preserves the industrial characteristics of the original building. The vaulted brick ceiling and structural pillars were kept intact, integrating a full-height steel-framed glass panel that divides the living area and studio from the bedroom and bathroom.

Architect: GCA Arquitectes Associats
Location: Barcelona, Spain
Date of construction: 2002
Photography: Jordi Miralles

Plan

Although the glass panel fully displays the bedroom, a curtain allows the space to become entirely isolated from the living area.

A quiet working and meeting area was situated behind the kitchen wall, a few steps up from the main level.

The large wooden panel behind the bed serves as a headboard, a bookcase and a divider that creates a separate space for the bathroom.

Private Loft

Architect: Sarah Folch
Location: Barcelona, Spain
Date of construction: 2002
Photography: Jordi Miralles

The integration of various levels can be very useful in differentiating the functions of a dwelling, especially when a space has the advantage of possessing high ceilings. The rectangular plan of this former industrial space combines all the areas into one, yet the layout achieves a clear distinction between the daytime and night-time areas by situating the bedroom on a slightly higher level.

Any hue can be easily added to a white space through the furnishings and introduction of colored accessories.

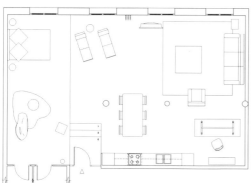

Plan

Ammann Apartment

The atmosphere of a loft can be established in many ways, without having to sacrifice intimacy. This apartment features a red unit, inserted into the living space, that contains the kitchen and integrates a series of closets for storage space. The bedroom is discreetly situated behind a white panel and enjoys direct access to a bathroom concealed within another box.

Architect: Delphine Ammann/N-body Architekten
Location: Frauenfeld, Switzerland
Date of construction: 2001
Photography: Reto Guntli/Zapaimages

The positioning of the bedroom behind a divider and adjacent to a black structure containing the bathroom bestows a great deal of privacy on the space.

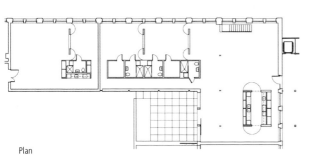

Plan

This small apartment takes advantage of the existing terraces to orient the living space in a way that maximizes daylight and views. By putting the living area and bedroom on elevated platforms, there is a perception of encumbered space is and a sense of differentiated zones. An unobtrusive curtain in the bedroom area allows for the choice of more or less privacy.

Architect: Ellen Rapelius,
Xavier Franquesa
Location: Sitges, Spain
Date of construction: 2002
Photography: Jordi Miralles

Plan

Within a small space, the furnishings should also serve the function of adorning the home, given the lack of space for decorative objects.

Architect: White Design
AB/White Architects AB
Location: Mobile
Date of construction: 2004
Photography: Bert Leandersonn,
Richard Lindor

Optibo

This project is an original proposal that provides a spacious residence within 270 square feet with the help of hydraulic and electrical systems. These technologies were applied to the various furnishings within the space, allowing allowing the main space to go from bedroom and living room to dining area and kitchen.

Plans

Plans

The hydraulic system open
and closes furnishings stored
in the floor. The electrical
system brings the lighting up
to the required intensity.

Various elements can be concealed underneath the floor, including the bed, tub, and table and chairs.

Designed as a home and studio for the well-known chocolate maker Enric Rovira, this apartment of just under 1,000 square feet makes use of a long, narrow floor plan to arrange a series of spaces that integrate closets and storage spaces along the lateral walls. The bedroom is integrated into the living area with its own wardrobe.

Architect: Francesc Rifé
Location: Barcelona, Spain
Date of construction: 2005
Photography: Eugeni Pons

Entire walls can be exploited for various uses by using wall units that combine storage and decoration.

Plan

The L-shaped working area comprises a tabletop supported by large, low cabinets that provide an additional working surface.

Given the relatively small
surface area, closets are
designed without handles so
they appear to be seamless,
uncluttered elements.

The focal point of this apartment is the versatile kitchen unit situated at its center. Measuring nearly five feet in height, the module is built with MDF and lacquered in white. It accommodates the kitchen, dining area and study, as well as providing shelving for the living room. The predominantly white space contrast with the black furnishings designed by the architect himself.

Architect: Francesc Rifé
Location: Igualada, Spain
Date of construction: 2005
Photography: Eugeni Pons

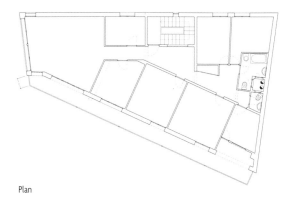

Plan

A spacious closet acts as a partition that separates the bedroom from the bathroom and other space.

The aim of this warehouse conversion was to embrace the structure's industrial history, maximize the entry of light, provide generous storage for daily use, and introduce new industrial materials for residential application. A full-height glass wall replaced a concrete balcony, cabinets were installed, and materials like epoxy, steel and recycled timber were used in revamping this space.

Architect: Greg Gong
Location: Melbourne, Australia
Date of construction: 2003
Photography: John Gollings

Hot-rolled steel panels used for the fireplace provide a unique natural pattern and decorative effect.

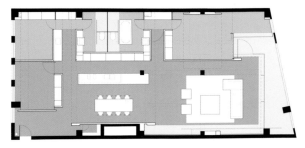

Plan

Epoxy floors all through the living areas reflect light in every direction, producing a lighter, brighter atmosphere.

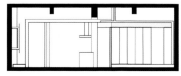

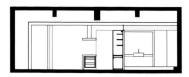

Sections

Freestanding units permit the
original concrete structure
and ceiling to remain intact.

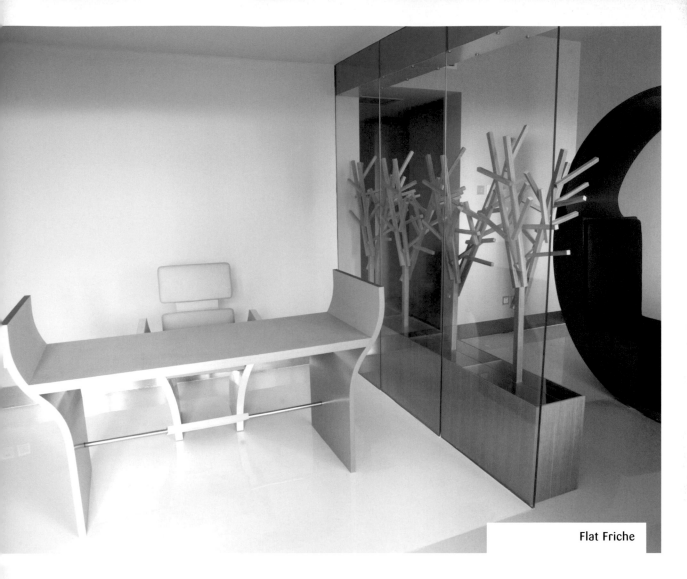

This apartment proposes an alternative way of living and perceiving the domestic space. Unique furnishings with peculiar forms that flow into one another challenge the conventional distribution of living areas within a home. Plantlike sculptures offer a welcoming vibe in the entrance, while more unusual elements include a miniglass house for aromatic plants in the kitchen and a meditation area next to the bedroom.

Architect: Matali Crasset
Location: Beijing Biennal, China
Date of construction: 2004
Photography: Matali Crasset
Productions

This colorful environment embraces a functional area not often designated in domestic spaces: a meditation corner for quiet contemplation.

Doppelhofer Apartment

This apartment in the center of Vienna was designed for a family of four and will be used eventually as a rental property for students. Divided into public and private zones, the space features a glass box that houses the bathroom. This box, in turn, serves as a dividing element between the living area and the bedrooms and incorporates an integrated wall unit.

Architect: Feyferlik/Fritzer
Location: Vienna, Austria
Date of construction: 2001
Photography: Paul Ott

A plastic curtain envelops the glass structure that contains the bathroom, offering privacy and establishing a visual boundary between living area and bedroom.

Penthouses

Pent Tank House

The renovation of a loft apartment and the repurposing of a room-size sprinkler tank on the apartments terrace resulted in this singular urban retreat overlooking Manhattan. In addition to restructuring the indoor living space, the roof deck was completely refurbished. The imposing cylindrical tank became, instead, a room for reading, relaxing and listening to music.

Architect: CSA Architects
Location: Sydney, Australia
Date of construction: 2004
Photography: Richard Powers

Flush panels were used throughout the apartment to lend a uniform quality to all the storage areas.

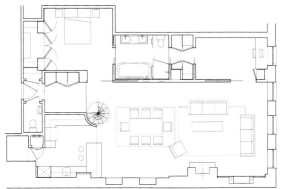

Plan

A skylight was introduced in the bathroom to create a spa-like atmosphere. Stone floors, polished waterproof plaster walls and a glass shower enclosure were also installed.

This spectacular apartment on the top floor of a former industrial building on the outskirts of Milan establishes a renewed dialogue with its historical context through the use of industrial materials and references. Neutral interior spaces were designed to accommodate the color-saturated midcentury modern furniture collection of the owners. A rooftop terrace with playful cutouts complements the interior.

Architect: Mauro Manfrin
Location: Milan, Italy
Date of construction: 2005
Photography: Andrea Martiradonna

A plain white space can come alive with the right choice and combination of furnishings and plants.

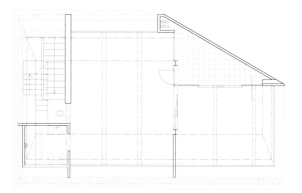

Plan

The internal ironwork was preserved as a
reference to the structure's original use
of an industrial building.

Red aluminium was chosen as an accent because of its frequent use in industrial buildings around the area.

Elliptical Penthouse

Arranged on the sixth and seventh floors of a prestigious new apartment building, this penthouse cleverly establishes a fluid, open-plan interior. Bedroom areas can be closed off with a series of concealed doors to provide seclusion when required. The top level is surrounded by glazed-glass walls that offer stunning views across the city. It opens onto a generous 1,350-square-foot terrace.

Architect: Form Design
Architecture
Location: London, UK
Date of construction: 2006
Photography: Mathew Weinreb

Ventilation ducts and other
installations are concealed
within the floor to minimize
visual interference.

A glass railing allows the occupants to see the upper living area from the open kitchen on the lower floor.

Milsons Point Apartment

This apartment was refurbished and conceived as a weekday home for the client, who spent extended weekends in their main house outside of Sydney. A reconfiguration of the space relocated the living area closer to the façade, and the kitchen was integrated into the main living area to benefit from the light and the views.

Architect: Stanic Harding
Location: Sydney, Australia
Date of construction: 2004
Photography: Paul Gosney

A built-in dining table doubles as a work area, highlighting the main purpose of this apartment.

Plan

A more private work area was created by raising it above the main level and giving it a different floor finish.

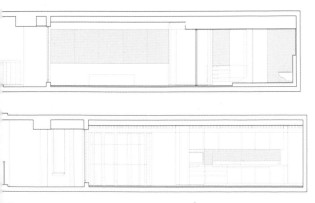

ctions

This apartment renovation entailed gutting and redesigning an three-bedroom apartment with views of the Sydney harbor. The architects' approach was to open up the traditional enclosed plan by fusing circulation paths with habitable space. An existing balcony was incorporated into the plan and transformed into a new dining area with all the benefits of an outdoor space.

Architect: Stanic Harding
Location: Sydney, Australia
Date of construction: 2002
Photography: Paul Gosney

An extension of the kitchen countertop functions as an eating area and also serves to mark the kitchen's separation from the living areas.

Plan

Left: Glass is used throughout to link the interior areas to the exterior. The glass provides views and adjustable louvers enable ventilation.

Slender

The architects who built this unique apartment atop a narrow building in the historic center of Berlin were challenged with a reduced 62 by 16 foot layout area. The residence was conceived as a series of functional spaces that flow into one another and culminate in a cantilevered structure that accommodates the bedroom.

Architect: Deadline Design
Location: Berlin, Germany
Date of construction: 2005
Photography: Ludger Paffrath

Simple materials such as
exposed and painted concrete,
throw the spotlight on the high
quality and structural elements.

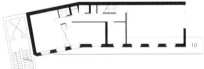

10

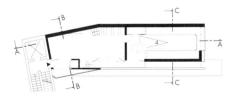

Plans

Contemporary fittings can be combined with other styles. In the bathroom, a romantic mirror functions side by side with an ultramodern washbasin.

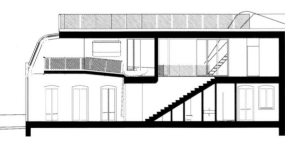

Section

This sophisticated luxury home provides a comfortable and cohesive setting for the display and enjoyment of the owner's extensive collection of artwork and antique furniture, and an eclectic mix of South African arts and crafts. Two entryways—one for the casual living areas and guest rooms; one for the formal living spaces—separate access to these two zones. They are joined together by a library.

Architect: SJB Interiors
Location: Melbourne, Australia
Date of construction: 2005
Photography: Tony Miller

The rooms within each zone were designed to heighten the duality of the apartment's character. The western section is more open-plan and the eastern section comprises more discrete, compartmentalized spaces.

Arresting naturalistic patterns and styles are juxtaposed to create a dynamic and interesting backdrop.

Shelving units are used to
display decorative objects as
well as to differentiate spaces.

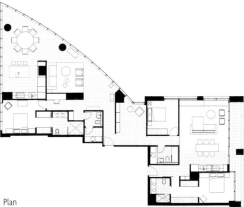

Plan

Architect: Blacksheep
Location: London, UK
Date of construction: 2004
Photography: Blacksheep

Yoo Building Penthouse

Situated in Maida Vale's former telephone exchange building, famously redesigned by Philippe Starck, this penthouse had to be planned according to the blueprint for all the apartments within the building, while still catering to the specific needs of the owner. Mirrors, smoked glass and bespoke furnishings make for a flexible and comfortable living space.

The living room features a
full-length voile curtain with
recessed LED lights for an
intimate atmosphere at night.

Antique furnishings, which
add character and warmth,
breathe life into this otherwise
minimalist apartment.

Plan

Behind the bed, a yellow
glass-mirrored wall allows
one-way views into the
kitchen, and increases the
daylight entering the room.

Chiswick Penthouse

Appointed by the client to create a tailor-made space with integrated storage solutions, the brief for this project was presented as a lengthy inventory of objects, including valuable artworks and a substantial library. A new central core and mezzanine were introduced to provide space for a home office, storage and glass-front cabinets in which to display the owners' collection.

Architect: Scape Architects
Location: London, UK
Date of construction: 2005
Photography: Kilian O'Sullivan

Plans

Lighting fixtures and
audio-visual equipment are
discretely concealed within
the ceiling and the seamless
arrangement of cupboards.

Unusual lamps can provide a distinctive
sculptural feature within any space.

The central white core
integrates a mezzanine level
with a working area that looks
out through the windows on
the exterior wall.

Walls harmonize with the
shapes and colors of the
paintings nearby.

Penthouse in Turin

Originally a nineteenth-century industrial premises, this spacious apartment conserves the existing stone and brickwork and integrates new materials that contrast with their raw appearance. The architect took advantage of the apartment's top-floor location by introducing various skylights into the space and making maximum use of the large terrace outside.

Architect: UdA
Location: Turin, Italy
Date of construction: 2003
Photography: Alberto Ferrero

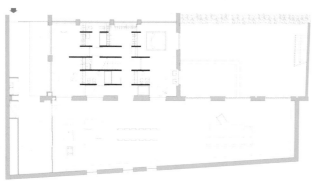

Plan

Fixed fastenings and doors
were fabricated of multilayere
birch that was coated with
anodized aluminium.

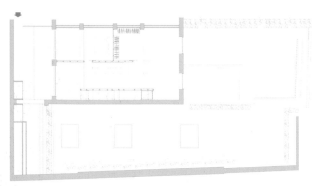

Plan

Polished concrete floors were chosen for the living area. Industrial wenge floorboards were selected for the bedroom and bathroom areas to bestow a feeling of greater warmth and comfort.

A previously dark and segmented floor plan underwent a thorough renovation to achieve a flexible layout with additional living space and daylight. A full-height glass wall inundates the living area with natural light and gives the occupants spectacular views of the cityscape. A restricted, neutral color palette and refined finishes generate an austere and elegant atmosphere.

Architect: Nadine Alwill
Location: Sydney, Australia
Date of construction: 2005
Photography: Murray Fredericks

Spotlights placed along the lateral walls can cast a soft light that produces an intimate and dramatic effect.

This top-floor apartment was reorganized to redirect the views from the living areas and obtain more hours of daylight. A new full-height glass wall delimits the boundary between interior and exterior spaces. A red wall defines the entry into the private areas, while also providing a series of closets, shelves and additional niches that serves as storage areas.

Architect: Riegler Riewe Architekten
Location: Graz, Austria
Date of construction: 2004
Photography: Paul Ott

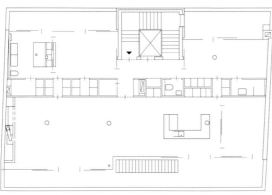

Plan

The use of wood along the interior and exterior floors creates a sense of continuity between both spaces.

The feeling of openness is
enhanced by the abundance
of mirrors and the glass
shower panel.

Glass Box

Architect: Eichinger
oder Knechtl
Location: Vienna, Austria
Date of construction: 2001
Photography: Margherita
Spiluttini

An old laundry on the attic floor of a building was converted into a small, luminous apartment. Existing partitions were removed, ceiling beams were covered with sheet metal, and the exterior wall was replaced with a large, folding glass window. Inside, a wire-mesh covering integrates cabinets and divides the different areas.

145

A motorized glass façade
opens up to create a balcony,
offering an exterior space
during the warmer months.

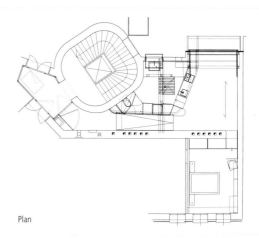

Plan

Translucent and reflective
materials are used to
maximize light, such as the
fine wire-mesh screen that
partitions off the bathroom
and shower.

L Loft

This rectangular space was transformed to create an open plan through the introduction of various materials, changes in level and mobile translucent partitions. Concrete, wood and glass are the main materials used to differentiate the areas of the residence, which makes use of existing elements such as the window opening and structural pillars.

Architect: William Ruhl/Ruhl Walker Architects
Location: Boston, MA, USA
Date of construction: 2004
Photography: Edua Wilde

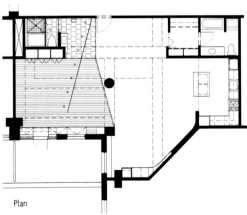

Plan

A translucent-glass wall cuts across the space diagonally to separate the living room from the master bedroom, which is also elevated on a wooden platform.

This residential project involved the remodeling of a dark and empty attic on the fourth floor of an eighteenth-century building in the center of Turin. The new staircase joining the apartment's two levels increases the flow of natural light, thanks to its clean, minimalist silhouette which transforms it into an ethereal element that does not interrupt the fluidity of the space.

Architect: UdA
Location: Turin, Italy
Date of construction: 2002
Photography: Emilio Conti

The glass staircase creates a minimal intervention in the transition from the lower level to the upper level.

Penthouse in Amsterdam

A standard apartment was transformed into a luxurious penthouse with a superb view of the city of Amsterdam. The glass expansion of the apartment is designed according to the rhythm and form of the original elevation. The new outdoor terraces are visually linked to the interior, which features an attractive contrast of light and dark tones.

Architect: Hofman Dujardin Architecten
Location: Amsterdam, Netherlands
Date of construction: 2005
Photography: Matthijs van Roon

Plan

A vertical kitchen cupboard creates a dynamic relationship between the kitchen and the living room.

Dark floors and splashes of color create a strong contrast with the crisp white walls and kitchen unit.